An Inner Journey to Easter

Lenten Devotionals
by Anne Kathryn Killinger

Smyth & Helwys Publishing, Inc.®
Macon, Georgia

For my sister
Mary Victoria
who is also my best friend

An Inner Journey to Easter

Lenten Devotionals

Anne Kathryn Killinger

Smyth & Helwys Publishing, Inc.®
Macon, Georgia

ISBN 1-57312-017-0

An Inner Journey to Easter
Lenten Devotionals by Anne Kathryn Killinger

Copyright © 1995
Smyth & Helwys Publishing, Inc.®
6316 Peake Road
Macon, Georgia 31210-3960

All rights reserved.
Printed in the United States of America.

The paper used in this publication meet the minimum requirements of American Standard for Information Services— Permanence of paper for Printed Library Materials.
ANSI Z39.48–1984.

Library of Congress Cataloging-in-Publication Data

Killinger, Anne Kathryn.
   An inner journey to Easter: Lenten devotionals / by Anne Kathryn Killinger.
   viii + 64pp.   5.25" x 8" (13.3 x 20.3cm.)
   ISBN 1-57312-017-0
   1. Lent–Prayer–books and devotionals. 2. Easter– Prayer–books and devotionals. 3. Devotional calendars.
   I. Title.
BV85.K47 1995   94-41131
242'.34—dc20   CIP

Cover design by Stephen Hefner

Scripture quotations are taken from the NRSV unless noted otherwise.

Contents

Preface ... vii

❧Transition❧

Day 1	Transition	1
Day 2	Pain	2
Day 3	Anxiety	3
Day 4	Sadness	5
Day 5	Fear	6
Day 6	Confusion	8
Day 7	Compulsiveness	9
Day 8	Change	10

❧Release❧

Day 9	Release	13
Day 10	Adventure	14
Day 11	Risk	15
Day 12	Achievement	16
Day 13	Protection	19
Day 14	Pride	20
Day 15	Rejection	21
Day 16	Apology	23
Day 17	Appreciation	25

❧Presence❧

Day 18	Presence	29
Day 19	Silence	30
Day 20	Beauty	31
Day 21	Reassurance	32
Day 22	Contentment	34
Day 23	Kindness	36
Day 24	Elation	37
Day 25	Support	38
Day 26	Worth	40
Day 27	Gifts	41
Day 28	Gratitude	43
Day 29	Blessings	44

❧Journey❧

Day 30	Journey	45
Day 31	Friends	46
Day 32	Hugs	48
Day 33	Forgiveness	49
Day 34	Compassion	51
Day 35	Words	53
Day 36	Time	54
Day 37	Justice	55
Day 38	Independence	57
Day 39	Faith	59
Day 40	Beginning	61

Preface

For a Christian, Easter is a very special time that should not to be approached casually or without any real preparation. Most of us prepare for it in casual ways. We think especially of what we shall wear: the old dress and shoes or new apparel, the familiar bonnet or a chic new hat. We usually plan a nice meal: ham or veal or turkey or lamb, yeasty bread, and perhaps a fattening dessert. Sometimes we even take a trip at Easter time to the mountains or seashore or to see family members who are dear to us.

If other people are like me, however, we often fail to prepare in the most important way: so that our hearts are ready for the dramatic news that Christ is risen and a new order is born! Easter sort of sneaks up on us. We know it is coming, but we get involved with all of the activities that usually keep us busy. Suddenly and without warning, it is here, and we are not spiritually ready.

We have not kept vigil through the long days of Lent. We have not walked with Jesus on his way to Jerusalem or watched and listened as he taught and ministered during Holy Week. We have not prayed with him in the garden of Gethsemane or followed him to the cross on Golgotha. When we wake up and realize that Easter is here, we feel empty, guilty, and unprepared for the blessing of a great celebration.

It does not take a lot of time to prepare for Easter; it requires only a few minutes each day. One of the best ways I have found to prepare is by reading something inspirational each day. I think it was Stephen Leacock, the humorist, who said that he liked to take small bites of thought and chew them well. It is amazing what a single idea or expression can mean to me when I lodge it in my heart and ponder it while going about my ordinary tasks and routines. Most of the writings in this book—one for each day during Lent—are ideas I have pondered in such a way. They are small thoughts or observations that I have enjoyed turning over and over in my mind, reflecting on their individual beauty, piquancy, or power.

I hope that reading and thinking about these selections will help you to prepare for Easter the way that writing them helped me. At the very least, I hope you and I will be friends when you have finished reading the book, for these are very intimate thoughts, and you will have spent several weeks with them. When we have made this inner journey, it will be my pleasure to wish you a happy Easter; and it will be my hope that your entire year will be richer and more rewarding for our having traveled this way together.

Anne Kathryn Killinger

❧Transition❦

I wish I were present . . . and could change my tone. (Gal 4:20)

Day 1

Spring arrived early this year. Rain has pelted the earth for six consecutive days. Our house is damp. The balmy temperature makes my skin clammy. Even my soul is moldy. What a way to begin Lent. If asked at this point what I'm giving up for the Lenten season, my quick response would be: "Rain."

With cabin fever and a watered-down soul, I decided to don some rain gear and brave the elements to take a three-mile hike. This daily walk is usually reserved for when my husband comes home from work. We enjoy strolling up and down the hills and chatting about the day's happenings. But today, facing the beginning of Lent, I needed to clip off the distance alone and try to find some redeeming feature to my being in a water-soaked world.

I've never enjoyed walking in the rain. As a child, I would be a "Miss Crossmouth" whenever I had to walk to school or church on rainy days. I had trudged along about half a mile, with my head bent low, before I realized the rain had stopped. "This is more like it!" I thought. A few minutes later, I felt a warmth on my back that made me stop and turn around. There was the mythical sun, barely breaking through a sky full of dark, ominous clouds. But that lone sun ray, shining brightly down on me, was like the breath of God giving me new life.

I resumed the walk with an uplifted heart and a bouncy step. Joyously, I began to see everything around me: the fat, wiggly earthworms; the smallest leaves on the tallest branches of the stately oaks; and the bunnies hopping from one green clump of grass to another. Gratefully, I admired the clusters of pure white blooms on the many wild dogwood trees beautifully gracing the wooded areas. The azaleas, tulips, and daffodils had been washed to the brightest reds, pinks, and yellows I had ever seen. I became heady with the sweet fragrance of the purple and white hyacinths brought out by the steady rains. The gentle wind whispered a delicate song of praise in my ears. It was as if everything in nature was preparing anew for a season of celebration to remember the passion, death, and resurrection of our Lord.

How will I celebrate Lent? I'm giving up a morose attitude and a dampened spirit. I'm taking a forty-day journey, hand-in-hand and tete à tete, with the Master. "The rain is over and gone. The flowers appear on the earth, the time of singing has come" (Song of Songs 2:11b-12a). Lent never began so beautifully.

Pain   Day 2

They led him away to crucify him. (Matt 27:31)

Pain is everywhere. It comes in different guises and degrees. Sometimes it is a mild interruption in a normal day, sometimes it is a constant companion. Pain is real.

Pain is frightening. It sends off alarms that can be difficult to shut off. Often it is a signal for help. A baby cries with an ear ache in the middle of the night. A child doubles over in pain from a ruptured appendix. A woman who is about to give birth emits a sharp, piercing noise.

Sometimes pain springs from a sense of lostness or from the hurt caused when loved ones are separated by war, death, or divorce. Some pain is excruciating. Think about the pain Mary must have experienced as she watched her firstborn son dying on the cross.

Transition

When our children were very small, we spent a month touring Spain. We visited many churches and museums, where we saw endless statues and paintings depicting the crucifixion. One day we noticed that our youngest son, then age three, was intent on drawing a picture of Christ on the cross. In one corner of the picture was a woman with great tears dropping from her face. I asked our son who the woman was. "That's Jesus' mother," he said. "She's crying. It must have hurted her."

The crucifixion "hurted" a lot of people, but it was necessary in order to change the world. It brought hope and meaning. It showed us that even pain can be a blessing.

Thank you, God, for the pain of your great sacrifice; for, through that pain, I have received eternal life.

Anxiety　　　　　　　　　　　　　　　　　Day 3

Therefore I tell you, do not be anxious about your life. (Matt 6:25)

More than once in the Sermon on the Mount, Jesus said, "Do not be anxious." I have thought about that statement for years. I have heard many sermons on it, read books and articles on it, and even given devotionals on it.

Unfortunately, I'm the kind of person who is anxious if she doesn't have some anxieties clearly in mind, and the very idea that I am not supposed to be anxious poses a real problem for me. My sister and brothers always said that our mother was never happy unless she was wringing her hands and worrying about something. Maybe that is why she so successfully raised a family of six overly anxious children.

I have discovered that there are degrees of anxiety. Maybe the three categories could be defined as gnat bites, a dog gnawing at the ankle, and being set upon by a pack of voracious wolves.

Small anxieties include worries about being punctual, choosing what to wear, getting the laundry done, unloading the dishwasher, marketing, deciding if it is time to color one's hair, and remembering to get gas in the station wagon before it runs out on the highway.

Medium-sized anxieties include such concerns as the dent in the fender, the trip to the dentist, the library book that is three weeks overdue, burning the roast thirty minutes before guests arrive for dinner, and forgetting to make motel reservations before a holiday weekend trip.

The real biggies are anxieties about serious illnesses, losing a job, moving, crime in the neighborhood, drugs in the schools, international justice, world hunger and poverty.

The problem for the anxiety-prone person is that worrying about even the most trivial concerns can become a total way of life. The anxieties pile up like immense snow drifts that block us from any hope of a peaceful, joyful existence. They govern our very being, turning us into martyrs, eroding our health, ruining our dispositions, and making us forget that the world is fun and beautiful.

My grandfather always insisted that some Bible verse says, "Fret not thy gizzard out." I have never located that passage, but there are some approximations of it. Though not quite as colorful as my grandfather's version, Paul's admonition is a great prescription for anxiety attacks.

> Do not worry about anything, but in everything by prayer and supplication with thanksgiving let your requests be made known to God. And the peace of God, which surpasses all understanding, will guard your hearts and your minds in Christ Jesus. (Phil 4:6-7)

Sadness — Day 4

Sorrow is better than laughter, for by sadness of countenance the heart is made glad. (Eccl 7:3)

Most of our days are so crammed with joy that we are irritated when clouds of darkness come along to rain on our parades. Yet we can't fully appreciate the experience of joy unless we have had to deal with sadness.

Sadness comes in many forms. Sometimes we feel it when we overhear a mother shouting at her child in a supermarket or see her slap the child in exasperation. Sometimes it occurs when we witness an owner beating a dog, and then see the dog lick the hand of the person who beat it. Sometimes sadness makes its approach through an elderly person who has been neglected, an AIDS victim who has been shunned by his or her parents, or a worker who has been unjustly dismissed from a job.

Of all the images of sadness I know, the most overwhelming is the picture of Jesus and the way he was treated. How unfairly people questioned his actions, used him for their own advantage, slandered his character, and finally beat and crucified him.

> He was a lamb
> Born in a world of wolves,
> And the wolves began to snarl when he was born.
> What makes us hate the innocent?
> What makes us restless till its heart is torn?
> A little lamb,
> A gift from God,
> And they hated him for even being born.*

How sad that we didn't learn anything from the experience of Jesus, that people still treat others the same way today. I feel that all sadness is related to the evil in the world and the way innocence is hurt.

How precious is the promise in the book of Revelation that in the world to come there will be no more sadness and no more tears. God will make atonement for all the hurt and injustice of this life and leave only love, kindness, and gentleness.

*John and Anne Killinger, "He Was a Lamb," © 1976.

Fear   Day 5

The fear of others lays a snare. (Prov 29:25)

I read a devotional today that offered an interesting method of dealing with fear. It suggested placing the fear in upturned hands and showing it to God, then turning the hands over and allowing the fear to drop out, and finally turning the empty hands upward so that God can fill them with perfect love.

I have so many fears that my hands wouldn't hold all of them. All my life I have been crippled by fear. Every day I feel as if I am skating on thin ice and that it will surely break and let me plunge into the cold, dark waters below. I am so habitually afraid that I can't conceive of ever breaking the habit. I live with my shoulders tensed, ready to ward off whatever comes. I seem to believe that if I am perpetually on guard I will manage to survive the worst life can offer.

Transition

Fear of life
Fear of death
Fear of losing
Fear of winning
Fear of traveling
Fear of staying home
Fear of responsibility
Fear of idleness
Fear of loving
Fear of not loving
Fear of God

I should have begun with fear of God. Growing up I learned at home and church about a God of fear and punishment. God would get me if I didn't do everything right, but I knew I couldn't do everything right. In fact, I was taught just the opposite—that I was a sinner, a klutz, a born loser. I could never please God by what I did. I was condemned from the outset.

I must reconceive my ideas about God. God is a God of love and forgiveness, of hope and celebration—at least for those who want to love God and do God's will. I must re-program my brain so that it stops sending negative signals. I must convince myself that God is really a God of love, and that perfect love really casts out fear. Maybe I'll begin by holding out my hands with my fears in them. If I can't get them all in, I'll do it again . . . and again . . . and again. I have a feeling this practice will make a big difference in how I face my day.

Confusion — Day 6

For God is a God not of disorder but of peace. (1 Cor 14:33)

Today my life seems to be at an all-time low. My mind continually flits from one thing to another, trying desperately to make sense of my feelings, to discover the reason for the confusion I am experiencing. Could it be the cross-country move we made? Am I still suffering from the empty-nest syndrome? Do I miss old friends? Am I spending too much time alone?

The questions tumble on, and the answers elude me. They tease me, then dart away when I think I am about to grasp them. My whole being is tired from this frantic search for solutions. I sigh constantly. I seem to be hurting and grieving for this trapped person inside of me who is so weighed down with confusion.

What is wrong? I have so much, but life seems empty. Sometimes I manage a little laughter, but it is like a momentary flicker of candlelight, easily extinguished by the great waves of melancholy that roll over me. While I'm bodily present to those around me, I am busy taking note of all the exits. I feel abandoned by family and friends. I feel abandoned by You. I'm not even present to myself.

Who wants to be around anyone who is so hopelessly lost and confused? What will it take to put my life in order again? I do want to get my priorities straight so that I can awaken each day and say, "This is the day that the Lord has made; let us rejoice and be glad in it" (Ps 118:24). I want my heart to overflow again, the way it once did, and to be able to say, "God is in heaven, all's right with the world"—and with this poor confused being of mine.

Compulsiveness — Day 7

For I do not do the good I want. (Rom 7:19a)

Many times I have heard the words, "Think before you act"—and almost as many times the words have gone unheeded. I am known to most of my family and friends as one who leaps ahead of anything slow-moving and must get right to the center of whatever is going on. I often act compulsively, without waiting to weigh the consequences.

Whenever anyone calls in distress, for example, my built-in computer begins immediately lining up a wealth of solutions to the problem. Without even hearing the end of the story, I want to rush in with brilliant advice. I chatter away compulsively, as if the mere quantity of wisdom I proffer will effect an immediate cure. Within minutes, I know I must have my poor caller hyperventilating and wishing she had not mentioned a word about her situation.

I also have a bad habit of finishing other people's sentences. I am so sure about what the conversationalist is going to say next that I can't resist the compulsion to seize the ball in midair and proceed to the nearest goal-line, leaving the bewildered person wondering what to say as a follow-up, lest I seize upon that and carry it away too.

Maybe these are not serious sins of compulsion, but they must surely be irritating to others. How much more thoughtful I would be if I only asked questions of the troubled person on the phone and gently led her to the conclusions about her situation that undoubtedly lie within her own grasp. How much more courteous I would be if I didn't interrupt other people's trains of thought by hijacking them enroute to their destinations. My compulsive behavior must signal a sense of superiority in interpersonal relations. I don't mean to send that message, but I probably do.

Compulsive persons like myself have an enormous amount of energy. We spring forth without much effort. It doesn't even take much to trigger the spring. Instead of devoting that energy to what appears to be the compulsive takeover of others' lives and situations, wouldn't it be wonderful if we could use it to be thoughtful and supportive of them?

Suppose we applied it to creative acts of listening—really listening—and to simply being there when others need us. Suppose we used it to exude understanding and caring when persons are troubled or distressed. Suppose we employed it to shore up their fallen defenses, encourage them when they are despondent about their own efforts, and remind them of how great they have been and how well they have managed on other occasions. Instead of supplying the answers for them, we would simply raise their self-esteem so that they could draw more easily on their own abundant resources.

I am trying to remember this little motto: "Give yourself quietly to others so that, instead of marveling at your strength, they discover their own." I think Jesus would have liked this saying. It was he who said, "Take my yoke upon you and learn from me, for I am gentle and humble in heart" (Matt 11:29).

Change   Day 8

He changes times and seasons. (Dan 2:21)

The world is changing every day, things are never quite what they were. Cities change, neighborhoods change, seasons change, families change, churches change, and friends change. Everything changes. I basically don't like change.

    I love visiting towns and cities around the world. I especially like to stroll down lanes where history was made, visit little museums, explore old churchyards with weathered gravestones, and discover little restaurants where the cuisine and the ambience are unforgettable.

    It bothers me to return to these places later and find that they have changed—to see buildings marred by graffiti or torn down to make way for new structures, to find quiet streets altered to make way for a McDonald's or a Kentucky Fried Chicken shop, or to discover that a church has been boarded up for lack of funds to maintain it. I want things to stay the way they were in my memories. I don't want to have to deal with a lot of alterations to the way the world was.

    Several years ago, my husband made a professional change that required moving from one part of the country to another. It meant a new house, new furniture, new friends, new shopping, a new schedule, and a new way of life. About the time of our move, one of our sons married, which meant more changes—a new daughter-in-law, new ways of relating, new arrangements for visiting.

    Some days I think my physical being is not geared to changes any more. There seems to be so many. Yet I love the changing of the seasons. Nothing thrills me more than crunching through dry leaves in the fall, watching a silent snowfall in the winter, smelling the freshness of spring, or feeling the stickiness of a summer day just before a thunderstorm. I can't imagine life without changes like these.

    I also think about the past changes in our lives. I've enjoyed all the places where we've lived. We have truly celebrated life in each place. I've loved the people we've known everywhere. What would I have done without them?

Why do I say now that I don't like change? Maybe it's because I never like to give up what has been but always want to keep things just the way they are. I feel a bond to all of the places I have been and people I have known. When any of them changes, I panic. The change threatens my life as I have known and loved it.

Yet I know that change is good. Think about the change that occurred when Jesus was born. Nothing has ever been the same since. Would I wish that away? Not at all. I suppose change is a necessary part of existence.

God doesn't change. God stays the same from one generation to the next. Change allows growth of the spirit, expansion of the mind, and flexibility of the heart. I simply must understand that and be prepared for change. Then perhaps I shall see it positively, as a condition for discovery and joy. I shall change, and then change will not seem so bad. Who knows? I may even learn to rejoice in it.

❧Release❦

You will be made free. (John 8:33)   Day 9

To release things—just to let them go, to resign control over them—is a tough assignment for me. I have a hard time releasing tension, stress, fear, or anger. My nature is to be in charge, to manage everyone and everything around me. Letting that control go is very difficult. Letting go means that many situations in my life will be unresolved and unfinished, situations that will never be set quite right.

Letting go means I will never have the good relationship with some people that I want—people who have steadfastly refused to get along, people who have willfully misunderstood, people I just wasn't on the same wavelength with. If I release them, we'll probably never be friends again, not with the depth and intimacy I desire.

Letting go means I'll have to stop struggling so hard with the church, which I dearly love but which gives me so much agony because it isn't the church I want it to be or that I believe Christ wants it to be. It's hard for me to let the church go on as it is and not live combatively with it, trying to remake it into my image of the ideal church. I have spent most of my life in a lover's quarrel with it.

I'm not sure I can let go. Letting go is probably the hardest thing I've ever tried to do. But what rewards it promises! If I release my tension, I will have more time and energy for meditation and the inner life. If I let go of my fear, I will be able to discover more of the grace and beauty in the world around me. If I surrender my need to redirect the thinking of my friends, I will have more love to give them. If I stop trying to remake the church, I will have more of a sense of worship and peace with God.

Jesus once told his disciples that if the people in a village refused to receive the word of the kingdom the disciples should merely shake the dust off their feet and go on to the next village. I remember someone saying that shaking the dust off our feet should have become a sacrament, like baptism and the Lord's Supper, so we would remember to do it. I'd like to try it now, during Lent, and see what effect it has on my life. I have a feeling it might even be miraculous!

❦❦❦

Adventure — Day 10

And Abram journeyed on. (Gen 12:9a)

Several years ago, I saw a play in which two young men were going into the city for adventure. Whenever anything unusual occurred after their arrival, the younger of them always innocently asked his friend, "Is this called an adventure?" Adventures are exciting and stimulating. They help us to relate to the greater life around us.

Recently I read a marvelous article in the newspaper about a man who is over 100 years old and is still attending college. He has earned many degrees over the years and has even been a college teacher himself, but his thirst for knowledge has never diminished. He reads three or four books at a time and says he feels that there is a new adventure waiting for him in each one of them. He lives with a thirst for discovery and understanding.

What happens to our understanding of people and the world around us when we aren't open to adventure? Our spirits so easily become stagnant when we cease to move outward, when we are content merely with the trips we have made in the past, when we stop trying to grow, when we cease to make friends beyond the little circle we have always known. Once we decide we have seen enough, learned enough, and experienced enough, the parameters of our lives begin to shrink, and soon all of life becomes a repeat performance for us.

It is easy enough to smile blissfully and dream of what was, but that is to arrest life where it was and miss all the great adventures God has in store for us ahead of where we have been. Jesus said, "I am the way, and the truth, and the life" (John 14:6). The way doesn't stop, it keeps going. Only as we continue in the way do we arrive at the truth and the life.

Going on is risky, of course. It is safer to stay where we are and be content with what we know. But maybe it is part of the subtle beauty of life that risk-taking almost always opens up new vistas to us and worlds we have never seen. Who knows? If we could take enough risks and see far enough, perhaps we could see everything the way God sees it!

Lord, please help all of your children to have the sense of adventure that led Abraham to leave home when you called him to enter the wilderness where you had wonderful things planned for him. Don't let us miss any of it!

Risk   Day 11
I will follow you wherever you go. (Matt 8:19b)

Life can be a dull and lonely business when we don't take risks. It's like hiding in a tunnel where we are safe but never tasting, seeing, hearing, feeling, or touching much of anything again.

What if Albert Schweitzer had never left his comfortable medical practice to go as a medical missionary to a primitive part of Africa?

What if Mother Teresa had kept within the safe compounds of her convent and only prayed for the lepers of India?

What if Handel hadn't given up his law studies to be a church organist and gone on to compose many great works such as The Messiah?

What if Michelangelo had been content to write poetry and hadn't gone forward to become one of the greatest artists of all time?

What if Mary and Joseph had not fled to Egypt to save their infant son?

What if the early Christians, knowing the fate that would befall them if they were discovered by the authorities, hadn't persisted in their devotion to Christ and preaching of the Gospel?

What if you and I play it safe and don't ever get involved with homeless people, or people with AIDS, or people of other racial backgrounds than our own?

Taking risks can be dangerous and disquieting, but risk-taking can also produce the most meaningful experiences of our lives. It can lead to a cross, as it did in Jesus' case, but it can also lead to resurrection.

Achievement — Day 12

This . . . must be fulfilled in me. (Luke 21:37c)

From an early age we are taught to be achievers. Parents urge us to do well in school and excel in athletics. Teachers expect us to reach our full potential as students and citizens. Peers admire us for doing well. The whole society tends to reward us for superior accomplishments. Even limited achievements are recognized. A two-year-old is applauded for tying his or her shoelaces. A Down's syndrome child is congratulated for participating in the Special Olympics. A ninety-year-old man is praised for qualifying for his driver's license again.

The accent on achievement, however, can be costly. I have seen ten-year-olds burned out by all the programs their zealous parents have urged upon them. Their after-school schedules are sometimes horrendous—piano lessons on Monday, horseback riding on Tuesday, dancing class on Wednesday, swimming on Thursday, soccer on Friday, crafts on Saturday, and tennis lessons on Sunday. They have no time to play and wonder and live like children.

Most of us adults impose the same kind of pressure on ourselves. We carry over from childhood the desire to excel, achieve, and be the very best we can be. We give 110 percent at our jobs, 110 percent at marriage and parenting, and 110 percent at buying and maintaining the finest homes money can buy.

Some of history's great achievements are enviable. How exciting it would be to paint like the great Impressionists, write poetry in the style of Wordsworth, compose cantatas with Bach's expertise, give concerts with the grace of Rubenstein, deliver an address with the oratory of William Jennings Bryan, or perform surgery with the skill of Michael Debakey. But most of us, for all our hard work, will never reach such heights. Although we are programmed all of our lives to succeed, we will never become famous for our achievements. What can we do? Is there consolation for us?

First, we can become great appreciators. At any ballgame, the spectators are as important as the participants. If they weren't there to see the game and cheer for their teams, the sport would be greatly diminished. The same is true in life generally. People who stand on the sideline and root for the competitors are as important in the overall scheme of things as the achievers themselves. Maybe we need to be taught this as children, while we are learning the value of achieving, so that all our lives we can be developing the art of appreciation.

Second, we can take "the long look" in life, viewing things from the perspective of eternity. This approach has a way of radically altering the meaning of achievements. Jesus told the story of a very wealthy man—and we assume, by the same token, a very important man—who, when he died, was judged by God as having been less successful than the poor beggar who lay at his gate, for the beggar was a man of faith.

Isn't it just possible that the only acclaim that really matters or has ultimate importance is the nod of approval from our Creator for what we have achieved from birth to death: "Well done, good and faithful steward" (Matt 25:21). Maybe this is what led the Apostle to say, after a life of spectacular achievements,

> Forgetting what lies behind and straining forward to what lies ahead, I press on toward the goal for the prize of the heavenly call of God in Christ Jesus (Phil 3:13b-14).

Protection — Day 13

> God is our refuge and strength, a very present help in trouble. (Ps 46:1)

My mother once said, "You can say anything you want to about Anne, but don't say a word against her husband or her children." These words rang true then and have remained unchanged these many years after her death. Somehow, in my eyes, my husband and sons have always been special people who should be protected from the world's cruelty and viciousness. For some reason, even with my limited capacity to protect them, I elected myself as their chief defender and have loyally fulfilled this self-appointment through the years.

I have fought, fumed, written letters, and wrathfully confronted people in behalf of justice for the three people who mean the most to me in this world. I am determined that these wonderful, God-fearing, and God-loving men shall be treated fairly and kindly by everyone around them. I am devoted to this role of protector of my family. Or, at least, I thought I was until I learned something at a recent dinner party.

After the meal we were seated comfortably in the living room with our friends. The wives were discussing the pros and cons of our husbands' vocations and places of employment. I voiced some dissatisfaction with some things about my husband's situation that I thought should be set right. Several other wives offered similar complaints about their husbands' situations. Eventually, the conversation moved on to other topics.

As our guests were leaving, one man said he wished his wife wouldn't always assume the mother's role of trying to protect him when things weren't going as well as they should. My husband, I thought, agreed a bit too eagerly. He also wished, sometimes, he said, that I didn't always get on my high horse about his causes.

I had a hard time going to sleep that night. I was struggling with my feelings on needing to keep the evil from my husband's and sons' doors. I realized that they have to fight their own battles and take the responsibility for their own conflicts. But what was I to do? For years, they have been at the very center of my life, and I have a fierce instinct to want to protect them. Finally, a sense of calm settled over me, and I uttered: "Thank you, God, for this insight."

I realized that my three men must act freely and individually. My role is to support them with a listening ear, loving arms, and prayers to God, whose ever-abundant strength is always theirs for solving their own problems. As much as I want to act in their behalf, there comes a time when a wife and mother can no longer do so. Like Hannah, the mother of Samuel, I must give my three men over to God, the real Protector, who will look after them far better than I can. I will surrender them to God, and then give thanks for everything.

Pride Day 14

The earth is satisfied with the fruit of thy work. (Ps 104:13b)

According to the Bible, "Pride goes before destruction." My mother used to say, "Come down to low doh, and don't be hifalutin."

I have always had a lot of trouble with pride and experienced a lot of confusion about it. When I was growing

Release

up, it was presented to me as negative and something to be avoided. The church hissed words of damnation upon those who were proud. My mother accused me of having dreams and ideas above my station.

I began piano lessons at age five. For years music was my life, my soul, my breath. I practiced for hours on end, striving to please my teacher. Mother said she had to drive me away from the piano bench, not toward it like ordinary children. I was enraptured by playing, by giving life to compositions, by allowing them to soar with beauty and glory. I was proud of my playing. More specifically, I had pride in it. I wanted it to be the best I could do. I wasn't satisfied with an inferior performance. I had to do justice to the beautiful scores of the great composers.

Was my pride wrong? I didn't think so then, and I still don't think so. My pride isn't personal or self-glorifying. It is pride in trying hard, in giving one's best, in refusing to turn in substandard performances, in renouncing slothfulness, in being true to the gifts of God. It means caring, loving, producing, sharing, and giving glory to God. My pride fulfills the biblical injunction, "Whatever your hand finds to do, do with your might" (Eccl 9:10a). The world needs more of this kind of pride. I need more of it myself.

Rejection   Day 15

He was despised and rejected by others. (Isa 53:3)

I was browsing in an elegant furniture and gift shop when I overheard a man asking two clerks if they had any bedsteads. They didn't understand what he was asking for and told him about the antique oak and pine beds they had in stock or others they could custom order for him. He kept saying, "No, I just want to look at some bedsteads."

Finally, someone in the store explained to the clerks that he wanted to see headboards. Their eyes opened widely, and they said they didn't stock those separately. Then one of the clerks dismissed him curtly with an added, "Go outside to smoke that cigarette." She didn't say "Please" or "I'm sorry," just "Go outside to smoke that cigarette."

The man's shoulders slumped as he turned to leave. He had not reached the door when the clerks and some customers standing near the checkout counter laughed at his simple way of talking. One of the clerks even made fun of the bibbed overalls he was wearing. Obviously, he was not accustomed to being treated this way. He just walked away, looking tired and bewildered.

The rejection that man experienced conjured up many thoughts in my mind. I reflected on the effects of shame, guilt, lostness, anger, helplessness, fear, and diminished self-esteem. Rejection can produce all kinds of negative outcomes. It can lead to loneliness, estrangement, or divorce. It can cause people to leave their jobs or commit crimes. It can even result in suicide. I firmly believe that rejection is the worst enemy that anyone can face.

When we visit England, we often go to the China Reject shops and sometimes to the Worcester factory that has an enormous warehouse filled with rejected dishes. The dishes and cookware in these places usually have tiny flaws in them—so tiny that you actually have to search to find them. They are marked down to very affordable prices. Through the years, we have completed whole sets of these dishes, bringing a few home at a time. Our friends think they are wonderful, but we know they have been rejected.

I wish the clerks who rejected that simple man in overalls could see the beauty in everything the way God does. If they could, they would never treat another human being that way again. They would realize that little flaws or differences make things even more beautiful and valuable—even themselves.

Thank you, God, for not rejecting me because of my imperfections.

Apology — Day 16

And they were greatly distressed. (Matt 17:23)

"I'm sorry." "Please forgive me." "Oh, I hope you will excuse me." I have a friend who constantly voices these little apologies. Her speech is peppered with them. She seems to feel that she is the sole originator of all errors in the world. If the Queen of England's four o'clock tea is cool, my friend knows that she caused it. It's almost as if she has to apologize for her very existence. Sometimes I fear she will be like the person I read about who said "Excuse me" once too often and was told, "I'm sorry, there is no excuse for you."

Doesn't one hear the most ridiculous excuses and apologies? Consider the ones people give for being late: "My dog was mad at me and wouldn't let me in my car." "My child was playing with all the clocks in the house and reset them wrong." "An elephant stepped on my foot."

How about the excuses given by sales clerks: "I'm sorry, madam, but that particular frock only comes in petite and extra large. If you would care for one in two-inch yellow and purple polka dots, I am sure we can find one in your size. If we don't have it in this store, we can get it for you in twelve weeks from our other store across town."

Then you hear explanations from mechanics: "We've run into a little problem on your car, sir. The whatzamajig had jammed itself against the whirlapin, causing a reaction in the whiffelsnort, so we've had to send for a whole new unit that won't be here until ten days from Tuesday. It will cost you a little more this way, but you wouldn't want to drive it without a new whiffelsnort. We'll call you when it's ready. Or, better yet, why don't you give us a call about this time next month if you haven't heard from us."

What I really long for is genuineness in the apologies I hear. I want to believe that people really mean what they are saying, that it sincerely grieves them to hurt your feelings, or run into your car, or be out of your favorite ice cream at the store, or cause you inconvenience by not having a part you need for your air conditioner. I would like to think that they are sorry enough to make some changes in their behavior in the future, to be more caring and thoughtful and helpful to others.

Then I think about my own apologies, especially the ones I make to God. Do I really feel repentant about the things I've done wrong? Do I really intend to make every effort to rectify my behavior and thought patterns in the future?

I'm sorry, God, if I have said things to you I didn't mean. Oops! There I go again. I hope I'm sorry. I really do. I don't want you to feel about me the way I feel about those other people who offer their cheap apologies.

Appreciation — Day 17

Love one another with mutual affection. (Rom 12:10)

Several years ago my sister's husband was in the intensive care ward of a hospital, hovering between life and death. Only his wife and children were permitted to visit him. It was a stressful time; if he died, he would be the first of the siblings or siblings' mates to leave us.

As I thought about him, I had a hard time remembering when he wasn't a part of our family. He and my sister married when I was only eight years old. The Christmas before they married he gave me a wonderful present. It had a Chinese checker board on one side and a regular checker board on the other. How I treasured that present! I felt a little sorry for my sister, to whom he gave only a hand-embroidered red robe. As my brother-in-law lay ill, I wondered if he knew how much that gift meant to me, but I felt it was too late for me to tell him.

After he and my sister were married, I spent many summers with them. Those were wonderful times, with picnics, camping trips, visits to the ice cream and donut shops, and lots of foods and pleasures I never had at home. But I can't remember ever throwing my arms around his neck and thanking him for expanding my world and giving me glimpses of life I wouldn't have had without him. Would it be too late for that? Even if I could have expressed my appreciation, he was too sick then to care.

Once, after I had married and my husband and I were struggling to make ends meet as we went to college, I was doing our laundry at my mother's house. It was a hot summer's day, and I was perspiring over the ironing board as I pressed my husband's shirts. For a long time, my brother-in-law watched what I was doing and said nothing. The next day he handed me a fifty-dollar bill and told me to take the shirts to the laundry for a while.

I am sure I thanked him at the time, but I never told him that money was so scarce for us then that I spent his gift on other things we needed more. He might have appreciated that. But I felt it was probably too late to tell him how much the money meant to us and how often I've thought about it and been grateful to him.

The years have come and gone. My husband and I raised a family. We often saw my sister and her husband and enjoyed our visits together. But I never really took time to sit down with my brother-in-law and talk about the things that mattered most to both of us. I just sort of took him for granted. I never listened to the story of his life as we went along, and I didn't tell him mine. As he neared death, I realized how much time had elapsed and how it was impossible to go back and redo the things we neglected. But maybe it wasn't too late for everything.

My brother-in-law survived. The following year after Christmas, we spent several days with him and my sister and had a wonderful time laughing and talking together. In fact, my husband asked, "Can we do this again next year?" Before our visit, my brother-in-law's mother had died and left him with a house full of furniture and accessories. While we were there, I helped to clean the house. My brother-in-law told me to take anything out of it I wanted. "Don't hold back," he said. We loaded a number of smaller items into the station wagon. As we were leaving, I hugged him and said, "I love you." He said the same to me.

I am grateful for the little remembrances of him that sit around our house. I treasure them even more, now that he too has died. I remember him each time I look at one of them. He will continue to live at our house through a vase, a lamp, a little table, or a what-not on the shelf.

The experience with my brother-in-law taught me a lesson. From now on, I will not wait to pass out my bouquets. I will be sure to tell people I love them while I have the chance to do so. I'll make certain they know what they mean to me.

Whenever I forget, Lord, get behind me and give me a little shove. I don't want to ever be too late again in expressing love and appreciation.

Presence

In your presence there is fullness of joy. (Ps 16:11) **Day 18**

Presence has many definitions. The one I'm thinking about is best described by something my brother said after a conversation with someone. "I was talking to Sam," he said, "and when I looked in his eyes, I realized nobody was home." The body was present; Sam's mind was elsewhere.

Nothing irritates me more than trying to talk to someone about an important matter when I feel that the person is not really with me. This treatment makes me feel that what I'm saying is too trite or obvious to deserve his or her attention. My spirit and confidence are diminished. I ask myself, "Am I boring? Am I offensive? Is what I am trying to say irrelevant? Is my presence embarrassing?"

Because this experience affects me so deeply, I shudder from time to time to think that I may be guilty of not being present to someone else. I may become preoccupied or careless and fail other persons in the very way that bothers me so much. Therefore, I must consider some rules for being present.

I must think about the hurt and harm my lack of presence can produce in someone else. I must count it an honor that other persons wish to confide their thoughts and feelings to me. I must understand that I am the real loser if I don't truly listen to others, because sometimes the simplest statement can carry the most profound meaning. I must remember invariably to listen to my heavenly Teacher, who always has time for everyone and has never failed to be there for me. He will instruct me in the deeper ways of presence. Presence, after all, is a gift.

Silence — Day 19

For everything there is a season, and a time for every matter under heaven: . . . a time to keep silence, and a time to speak. (Eccl 3:1, 7b)

When our children were growing up, the most difficult role I sometimes had to play was that of remaining silent. It would have been so easy to give them all the answers, even before they asked any questions. I could have made all their decisions for them, even before they reached the crossroads. It wouldn't have cost me much or been nearly as hard as staying quiet. Fortunately, somewhere along the way, I learned the importance of not interfering.

One time our son needed a new pair of glasses. He tried on frame after frame. Suddenly he stopped. I almost opened my mouth in horror to say, "Oh, son, not those! You look terrible in wire frames." But I didn't. I noticed the glow on his face. "These are the ones, Mom," he said. "Aren't they great?" He made a choice, and I realized I had to give him the right to enjoy his decision, even if it meant I thought he looked ghastly until time for another pair of glasses. His ability to make decisions for himself was the important issue.

Years later our other son was due home from college and I was rushing from a meeting to greet him. As I drove along the street near our house, I noticed a young, long-haired runner with a bandanna tied around his forehead. He had a beard and was wearing ragged, cut-off jeans and an old sweat shirt that was more full of holes than Swiss cheese. Some mother, I thought sympathetically, must be really upset at the way her son goes out in public. The thought had barely crossed my mind when suddenly the truth registered: "That is my son!" How I wanted

Presence

to stop the car and lecture him about his appearance. Instead I reflected and realized that he had the right to discover his own identity and learn to take responsibility for the self he would grow into. I think I did a far better thing by stopping the car, throwing out my arms, and saying, "Welcome home, son!"

Love often made me bite my tongue and remain silent. My children really needed hugs and affirmation more than they needed my advice. Now that I think about it, I realize that God is often silent, too. When we make mistakes, or think the wrong things, or go at life with twisted methods, God must really want to say something to us or reach out and turn us in a new direction. But God remains quiet, like a loving parent, and waits for us to find the way by ourselves. This is the divine tribute to the way we are made and to the relationship we have to the eternal. God allows us make our own decisions, like the prodigal son, but God is always there, like the loving parent in the story, to welcome us home with open arms.

Beauty   Day 20

Let the beauty of the Lord our God be upon us. (Ps 90:17a)

> For the beauty of the earth,
> For the glory of the skies . . . .

How marvelous it is to wake up in a sunfilled room and know that the day is going to be full of miracles! That must be the way a child wakes up every day. The child enters the world each day to experience it without any preconceived ideas of how everything must turn out.

My husband and I were hiking through the woods in a state park recently when we overheard a young father pointing out the wonders of the forest to his four-year-old son. He talked to him about the pine cones, the squirrels, the violets beginning to appear from beneath the leaves, and the deer that occasionally showed themselves by the stream. Suddenly, the father noticed that the son wasn't saying anything. "Son," he said, "aren't you listening?" "Oh yes, Dad," replied the son, a tone of admiration in his voice, "I beweave everything you tell me."

The beauty of innocent, trusting love! My heart cries out for a simple, uncomplicated way of seeing the world, so that I too may respond like a child. I want to live in awe on this thrilling stage where God has set us to act out our lives. I want reverently to discover:

> All things bright and beautiful,
> All creatures great and small,
> All things wise and wonderful,
> The Lord God made them all.*

Lord, I want to "beweave" in everything!

*Cecil Frances Alexander, "All Things Bright and Beautiful," 1848.

Reassurance   Day 21

[God] has given assurance to all. (Acts 17:31)

All my life I have craved the reassurance that I am loved and accepted. I could never get enough hugs and verbal acceptance from my parents. Now it is the same with my husband. "Do I look all right?" and "Did I say the correct thing?" are only the beginning of the many questions I have plied him with over the years.

For years, my husband thought these questions were asked out of vanity, because I wanted to hear myself praised. I think he was actually stunned when he realized that vanity had nothing to do with them, that I was so truly lacking in self-esteem and confidence that I needed constant assurance of my worth as a human being.

I have prayed the same prayer for reassurance so many times through the years that God must wonder if I spend all my time and energy focusing on myself. But it is so important to me to feel that I'm okay and accepted as a part of everything around me.

A few years ago we attended an engagement party for our son and his fiancée at the fiancée's home. With my usual sense of agony over whether I was saying the right things and conveying the right impressions, I was glad when the party was over, and we could escape to the safety and quiet of our room.

The next day our son's future mother-in-law called to invite us back for leftovers. She and I were in the kitchen together while the food was heating. She stopped what she was doing to announce to me that this wedding didn't belong just to her family, but that my family was to be included in the planning and preparations, too. She made me feel comfortable about my role as the groom's mother. I went home feeling reassured that I was really necessary to the wedding and not merely a bothersome extra that people had to maneuver around.

It's so wonderful to feel that I am a part of the whole, to have the reassurance that there is a place for me. Sometimes I'm glad to feel unique and different from other people, but most of the time I want to belong and know that I am accepted.

I really admire Jesus, when I think about it. His ministry was to the people who felt unacceptable among others: publicans, prostitutes, lepers, and other outcasts. He claimed that he was doing the work of his Father in heaven. Maybe that's what heaven is all about: feeling totally, utterly, completely accepted by everybody else who is there. Won't that be something!?

Contentment — Day 22

I have learned to be content with whatever I have. (Phil 4:11b)

Contentment with whatever we have is a beautiful thought, but a hard attitude to achieve. On a rainly day, most of us wish for sunshine, or, if we have had a lot of sunshine, we wish for rain. If we're eating a meal that isn't quite up to par, we wish for the one that was so good when we had it last week. If we're on the East Coast we dream about being on the West Coast, and if we're out West, we can't wait to get back East. If there is something we don't like about the church we attend, we wish for another one. Some of us change jobs again and again, trying to find the one that is just right. We're all looking for Utopia, our own beautiful, blissful Camelot.

What a shock to reach one's middle or later years and discover that he or she is still searching for the perfect place to be, the perfect house, or the perfect mate. How much of life's precious time we waste by always looking for something better and not enjoying the challenges and rewards of where we are and what we have. We skim along on the mere surface of life instead of digging in and discovering the joy and excitement of our present possibilities. We spend our lives looking for the end of the rainbow, when it really lies in our own backyards.

I think about my son, an extraordinarily talented artist. The extent of my own artistic fame was reached in an art education class in college when I drew a dog that the professor thought was a pig. I am not diminished by the fact that I am not an artist. I can appreciate my son's art.

Once, when we were strolling down a street in Colonial Williamsburg, we heard a beautiful soprano voice coming from one of the taverns, gracefully singing music from the early period in America. I greatly admired the voice, but I am content with the warbly alto voice I have.

Some people amaze me with the feats they can accomplish at the computer console: solving puzzles, making graphs, developing formulas, and creating beautiful designs. But I do not have to imitate what they can do. I can be happy with a reasonably good handwriting and a little skill at a typewriter.

There are wonderfully fascinating places to live all over the world. I enjoy visiting them and reading and seeing travelogues about them. But this does not mean that I can not still be happy even if I don't live in those places. I enjoy my own home and community and am content to enjoy the other places vicariously.

God has given us a remarkably rich and diverse world, and it would be wrong of us to spend our lives longing for what we cannot have or trying to get what we do not possess. We can be content with knowing it is there and praising the Creator for it. After all, God is reflected in all of the world, and our greatest desire is for the Creator, not for some limited part of creation. Maybe this was Paul's secret. He was so happy with God that nothing else mattered much anymore. That's real contentment!

Kindness Day 23

God is slow to anger and abounding in steadfast love. (Joel 2:13)

One rainy day when my husband and I were in Gatlinburg, Tennessee, and couldn't hike in the mountains, I spent the time with two of my favorite pursuits: shopping and people-watching.

In a clothing store, I noticed an attractive-looking couple at the sweater counter. As I drew closer, I realized they were having a quarrel. The man was using terribly abusive language to the woman, and she was begging him to please be nice this one time. Her distress appeared to spur him on to even harsher behavior. I was so disquieted by the scene that I had to leave the store.

Later, I stopped in a shop for some frozen yogurt. A mother and her two small boys were in line ahead of me. She asked the older boy what kind of yogurt he wanted. The smaller boy, who looked to be about four years old, spoke up and said he wanted chocolate. Wheeling around, the mother slapped him in the face and said, "Shut up! I'll order for you!" The clerk and I looked on in amazement, unable to believe that a mother could behave so cruelly toward that beautiful, upturned face with wide, excited eyes.

Fortunately, I saw a lot of positive interchanges as well and can testify that they far outweighed the negative occasions, such as the father who gently cradled his small son who had fallen down.

My heart was warmed by the patience and kindness a middle-aged mother showed her Down's syndrome son. He was looking at CD's in the record store, and she suggested ones she knew he liked, and asked, "Is that one all right with you?" His face would light up in agreement, and he would give her a hug, which she never failed to return.

In one store, a child was purchasing a toy. He asked the sales clerk the price. When she told him, he counted his money and found that he was a few cents short. His little shoulders slumped in disappointment. Another shopper overheard and stepped to the counter. She said she had some extra pennies that were just waiting to be given to a nice little boy. The child's smile seemed to light up the entire store!

Kindness is so easy to give, and it is so good for us. Nothing else makes the heart lighter or does so much to remove wrinkles. A lack of kindness, by contrast, comes from a withered soul. They are both contagious. I love the motto, "Smile and the world smiles with you."

We have a wonderful model in our Lord, who befriended the meek and helpless and encouraged little children to sit on his lap. When we are kind and good to others, we allow the world to see him again through us. Even on a rainy day, he makes the sun shine in our hearts.

Elation — Day 24

> They sang praises with gladness. (2 Chron 29:30)

I feel elation this morning. I awoke to bright, glorious sunshine. The whole world was smiling after several days of mist and darkness. When I came downstairs for breakfast, John's warm arms encompassed me, and I felt safe from any outside intrusion. With such a loving, positive beginning, what else could one feel but elation?

An impromptu idea came to my mind at breakfast. I shocked John by suggesting that we fly to England during his spring break. He said it was a great idea, but the break was too short. Why not go in May? I called the different airlines for schedules and prices. Maybe we'll follow through and maybe we won't, but it was a time of elation for both of us.

Elation, joy, and excitement have been missing for a long time from our cluttered lives. It's as if I've been punishing myself by not allowing room for them. I don't really enjoy self-flagellation, but I have surely indulged in it.

Now I'd like to cut loose from all of that and go on a binge of happiness and enthusiasm—just blow everything on a big, wall-to-wall party. Maybe I'll pay for it later in feelings of guilt and recrimination, but I'll face that when the time comes. For now I want to live, I want to feel joyous, I want to celebrate, I want to experience elation.

Isn't that what faith is about, feeling elated without guilt? Doesn't the truest sense of elation we ever feel come from standing in the presence of God? Then I want to be elated now, every day. I want this mood to continue. It's the way my life ought to be—not dull and plodding and filled with clutter, but bright and shining and effusive with happiness. I'm glad I realized this, it adds to my elation!

Support   Day 25

We urge you, beloved, to admonish the idlers, encourage the fainthearted, help the weak, be patient with all of them. (1 Thess 5:14)

An old African-American spiritual says, "Build me up where I have fallen down, prop me up on every leaning side." Everyday, we have opportunities to lend a hand to someone who needs support.

Presence

Several years ago I was assigned to the surgical ward while I was serving as a volunteer pink lady at the hospital. The waiting room was always filled with people anxiously awaiting word from their loved ones in the operating room. Anything I could do for them was meaningful, whether it was giving them a touch or a hug, speaking a word of reassurance, or getting them a cup of coffee. Even a token amount of support was helpful.

In a sense, that hospital room was the world in microcosm. We are surrounded by hurting, anxious people, by people who need to be propped up on every leaning side. We can help others in so many ways.

We can listen to friends when they need someone to talk to and provide loving concern and encouragement.

We can visit people who have been ill and take food and flowers to cheer them up.

We can take little gifts to those who live in retirement homes or are confined for reasons of age or physical infirmity to their own homes.

We can volunteer to sit with hospital patients while their family caregivers run necessary errands or just get away for a little while.

We can make a point of including divorced persons in our social agendas, so that they won't feel isolated and alone after the trauma of separation.

We can go out of our way to be kind and thoughtful to young people who are having a problem with drugs or alcohol, so that they have someone to turn to in their hours of deepest need.

We can be kind and sympathetic to people we meet in the supermarket, drugstore, or mall.

I recently met a lonely young man while waiting for a table in a restaurant and listened as he told compulsively of his dating problems and personal hangups. I did little to alleviate his distress—except to lend an attentive ear. He was profusely grateful, as if he had been desperate for another human being with whom to share his story.

A smile, a nod, a wink, a little shrug of the shoulders, a touch on the hand, an embrace, a kiss—these are small and inexpensive gestures of love and support, but they mean so much to persons to whom we give them. There is a side-effect: When we prop others up where they are leaning, our own foundations become more secure.

Worth — Day 26

Our God will make you worthy of his call. (1 Thess 1:11)

It always seems to amaze people when they discover that I do my own housecleaning. If they question me about it, I jokingly reply, "I have to justify my existence." Maybe there is more than a grain of truth in that response. I do feel more worthwhile when I have dusted a floor or scrubbed a shower stall. What really constitutes worth?

I recently visited a friend who is in a mildly depressed mood. Always a busy, work-oriented person, he has been troubled lately because he doesn't think his life counts for much. He holds Mother Teresa as a model for the way his life should be and worries that he has not contributed to society in the way she has. Several times in our conversation he said, "I want to be worth something, to do some good." He is a good man and has meant a lot to many people, but he is not convinced of his value. He wants to do something of real importance, something outstanding and dramatic.

All of us would like for our deeds to make history the way Mother Teresa's have. We would like to know that our contributions rank with those of great composers, inventors, artists, and statesmen. But we feel lost in our tiny, uneventful corners of the world. We bemoan the fact that no matter what we say or do, it will not make a significant difference. We say that we are not worth anything, but this is simply not true.

Every person's contribution, regardless of how small it may seem, is important in the overall scheme of things. My friend is doing something worthwhile when he dusts a floor or cleans a shower stall for his family. Maybe he cannot go to Calcutta and work with Mother Teresa, but he can pray for her and the success of her work. The thousands of people who support Mother Teresa with their prayers and donations are just as vital, in the eyes of God, as she and those who labor at her side.

Emily Dickinson summed the matter beautifully:

> If I can stop one heart from breaking,
> I shall not live in vain;
> If I can ease one life the aching,
> Or cool one pain,
> Or help one fainting robin
> Unto his nest again,
> I shall not live in vain.*

*Favorite Poems of Emily Dickinson (New York: Avenel Books) 24.

Gifts   Day 27

Every perfect gift is from above. (Ja 1:17)

This is an unusually bright, beautiful morning. Nature is awakening with red-bud and fruit trees. Tulips, daffodils, and azaleas are bursting forth in vibrant colors. The birds seem to welcome these signs of spring with melodic rapture. Even the smell of the early morning breeze touches off signals in the body that make one aware of all the fantastic gifts God has given us:

ordinary gifts
extraordinary gifts
surprising gifts
unsurprising gifts
demanding gifts
undemanding gifts

On this perfect day, it is so easy to take all of God's gifts and simply revel in them. Happy, happy, happy. But something is gnawing at the edge of all of this happiness. It whispers: "What are you doing with the gifts God has entrusted to you?"

I respond: "Go away, thought processes. Go away, responsibility. I want to bask in the joy of this moment. I want to luxuriate in the freedom of this experience."

But the gnawing continues. Every time I try to snuff out the voice, its volume increases. "Use your gifts for God and God's children. They were given to you to develop and use, not to be put on a shelf and admired."

The struggle ceases only when I realize that it is all right to enjoy the wonderful gifts God has given me if I reciprocate by trying to cultivate my personal gifts and employ them unsparingly for God's own enjoyment and fulfillment. The gift tags must read: "To me, with love, from God." "To God, with love, from me."

Gratitude — Day 28

We always give thanks to God. (1 Thess 1:2)

"Thank you" is something we say so often that it almost loses its meaning. It is an automatic response we make to waiters who bring our food, to persons who hold the door open for us, to clerks who locate items we couldn't find in the store, or to members of our families who surprise us with gifts. It may be said with enthusiasm, grudgingness, amazement, or sarcasm. However it is said, it is said almost constantly—and appropriately so.

We have so many things for which to be thankful:

God
life
families
love
happiness
beauty
learning

The list is endless—as endless as my gratitude on this day thirty years from the day our youngest son was born.

When I think of the challenges and happiness that son has given me through the years, there isn't enough time or space to contain all the thankfulness I feel. My thank-you for him is not coming from some automatic response or some casual and unthinking reaction to his existence. It resounds in my heart and soul, like a great symphony that grows in intensity until it threatens to burst out of its container and fill all of the open space. God understands; God had a rare and beautiful son too. Thank you, God, for both of them.

Blessings

Day 29

> [The earth] receives a blessing from God. (Heb 6:7)

"Count your blessings, name them one by one." I grew up singing that old hymn. It had a lively tune, and the words were simple for a young girl to sing. But I can't recall ever really contemplating its message.

"Count your many blessings, see what God has done." It was enough, then, to sing in the church choir or just be with those comfortable people in the congregation. I didn't really need to enumerate my blessings. Now that I'm older, though, I do need to enumerate them. I have traveled enough and seen enough both at home and abroad to know how lucky I am to be warm, well fed, and healthy.

Blessings from God: I have worked with adults who could not read or write and know how fortunate I was to go to school and learn as a child.

Blessings from God: I have a friend who is blind. She is wonderful and courageous, and puts many of us who are sighted to shame. But her world is so much more circumscribed than mine.

Blessings from God: Friends have died of cancer, AIDS, and other dreadful diseases, and they have made me more aware of the beauty of life itself.

Blessings from God: I have seen broken homes and homes where there is little love, and realize how important my husband and children have been to me.

Blessings from God: My world has been unspeakably rich in both people and things. I cannot begin to count all of them. I can only sing, "Praise God from whom all blessings flow!"

Journey

> He went on his way through towns and villages, teaching and journeying toward Jerusalem. (Luke 13:22 RSV)

Day 30

Some people love to plan trips. They pour over travel books and maps day after day, dreaming of faraway places, but never get around to actually going anywhere. They reason that the trips are too expensive, or perhaps they will become ill while traveling. They play the "what-if" game and stay home, missing out on wonderful adventures.

Some persons live their professional lives in a similar way. They spend long hours at the office or burn the midnight oil at home thinking about great plans for the future that would lead to job promotions or moving to a large city. But they never carry out these plans because of the pitfalls they might encounter in doing so. They remain in their safe surroundings and wait for retirement.

Some of us continually brainstorm about the things we ought to be doing for God's little ones. We imagine how we could change life for the underprivileged. We mentally arrange programs to feed the hungry. We design suitable shelters for the homeless. We contemplate ways of eliminating prejudice from society. We are full of plans, but we seldom do anything because we don't want to take the risk of confrontation or failure.

The single thread running through all of life's nonoccurring journeys is the fear that something unpleasant might happen. But something unpleasant can also happen when we are merely playing it safe. We can miss out on the growth and excitement that come through making a real journey.

As someone who had a hard life once said, "God didn't promise us an easy way; he only promised us a safe arrival at the end." Wouldn't it be wise, therefore, to embark on as many real journeys as possible? Even if there are risks along the way, we know they will all end safely in God. Happy traveling!

Friends   Day 31

A true friend sticks closer than one's nearest kin. (Prov 18:24b)

Isn't it wonderful to have the love and support of friends? Once, my brother-in-law was in critical condition in a hospital many miles from his home. His daughter was staying with him. My family and I had once lived in the city, so I phoned an old friend and asked her to check on my relatives and give them the support they needed.

This friend visited the daughter several times, giving her moral support and encouragement. Once, she even prepared lunch and took it to her at the hospital. After each visit, she called us with a report of my brother-in-law's progress. She was an invaluable help in a difficult time, like the good Samaritan in Jesus' story.

Friends wear many hats. Some are saints. Their endurance level goes beyond the imagination. No matter how much abuse they suffer, they continue to wear sweet smiles and speak encouraging words. They are our Christian role models.

Other friends are missionaries. When we are ill or have experienced tragic events, they are the first at our doors with homemade chicken soup and a basket of flowers. Their message is that God cares and so do they.

Journey

Many friends are musicians. They seek harmony in personal relationships. They are even skilled at working miracles with tone-deaf choirs.

Perhaps the friends who are most appreciated are the unselfish financiers, those who give generously to the poor, hungry, and disadvantaged of the world. They know full well there will never be any monetary return on their investments, but they take seriously Jesus' command, "Feed my sheep" (John 21:17).

Surely the best friend anyone can have is the sacrificer, the one who is willing to undergo any amount of personal pain and injury in behalf of someone else. Jesus was this kind of friend. He gave up everything for me. When I think of him, I remember a little song I learned as a child. It said, "My best friend is Jesus. Praise him. Love him. Serve him." His goodness and kindness to me make me want to pray the prayer of Patrick of Ireland, written in the fifth century:

> Christ be with me,
> Christ within me,
> Christ behind me,
> Christ to win me,
> Christ to comfort and restore me,
> Christ beneath me,
> Christ above me,
> Christ in quiet,
> Christ in danger,
> Christ in mouth of friend or stranger.

Hugs

Day 32

[There is] a time to embrace. (Eccl 3:5b)

Arms are for hugging. At least, that's what I told our boys when they were very small, and now that they are grown men, they are the best huggers around. Hugs from my family and friends mean a great deal to me. They assure me that I am loved and secure. They are a comfort when the most devastating events occur. Hugs are surely a blessing from God.

One of the most important hugs of my life came while my husband and I were serving a church in Los Angeles. After the annual community Thanksgiving service, most of the people had hurried off to prepare the feast of the day. A few of us were still standing around, chatting and feeling good that we had experienced a meaningful service and were looking forward to further celebrations of the day.

I looked away from the group and saw a dirty, ragged, pitifully thin man coming toward us. I suggested to the group that we move and not deal with another street person that day. After all, it was Thanksgiving. But the man followed us. Confrontation was unavoidable.

He didn't ask us for money, though he asked if he might have a drink of water. Finding pity in our hearts, we got him a cup of coffee and led him into the building, where it was warmer. He told us that he had AIDS and didn't have long to live. His parents had turned him out when they learned about his condition, and he was sleeping on the streets and eating out of garbage cans. Someone had beaten him and stolen his shoes. His clothes were stained with blood. I looked at his poor feet, covered with socks and plastic bags.

He began to cry, and I put my arms around him. He said it had been a long time since anyone had hugged him. He asked if he might kiss my cheek. By that time, we were both crying. I continued to hold him and rock him, the way I had once rocked my own boys. Finally, we called the AIDS shelter, where he would receive a friendly welcome, a clean bed, and a wonderful Thanksgiving meal. My husband phoned for a cab and instructed the driver about where to take him.

When our boys were growing up, and I knew they had something especially difficult to deal with, I always sent them off to school with a hug, a kiss, and a reminder: "My arms are around you." I thought about that as I watched the poor, frail man shuffling off to the cab. I thought, "My arms are around you, too." I had received a hug I would never forget.

I pray that the Thanksgiving man suffering with AIDS is now with God, forever enfolded in the arms of the One who will never discriminate against him, persecute him, or abandon him. What did Luke say in his Gospel? "The poor man died and was carried to Abraham's bosom" (Luke 16:22a).

Forgiveness   Day 33

If you forgive others their trespasses, your heavenly Father will also forgive you. (Matt 6:14)

A female member of a large family set about systematically destroying the relationships within it. She made telephone calls to several brothers and sisters with malicious stories about another brother and his wife. Then she called that brother and his wife and told them the bad things the rest of the family were saying about them. That brother's wife became very upset and immediately telephoned the other family members. Without giving them a chance to tell her they hadn't said or done anything to harm her and her husband, she made angry statements to them and ordered them never to come to her home again.

The rest of the family was bewildered and shocked by all of this. They loved their brother and his wife and could not understand what was happening. After two years of this unsettling "feud," all of the family members were brought together by the hospitalization of their elderly father. In the exchange that followed, they discovered what evil the one family member had perpetrated, and everyone made peace with the sister-in-law who had spoken so angrily to them. She kept saying, over and over, "Can you ever forgive me?" They did forgive her and assured her that they did.

The entire family was happily reunited—except for the one member who had caused the trouble in the first place. She was unrepentant. She did not ask to be forgiven. She didn't learn anything from the pain she caused. She continued trying to sow seeds of discord in the family.

This kind of behavior is not new. In fact, it is as old as recorded history. Cain murdered his brother Abel. Jacob stole the birthright from his brother Esau. Joseph's brothers sold him into slavery. The older brother in Jesus' story of the prodigal son despised his brother and resented his return to the father's love.

Unfortunately, troublemakers are not found only in families. They are also in churches, schools, clubs, corporations, and communities. These people are always stirring up hatred and unhappiness, discontent and resentment. The wounds they inflict on the hearts of others are often slow to heal. Sometimes the scars never go away.

The people who sent Jesus to the cross were troublemakers. They were cruel and thoughtless. It is almost unthinkable that people should be forgiven for such things. Yet, even as Jesus was dying on the cross, he said, "Father, forgive them, for they do not know what they are doing" (Luke 23:34).

Somehow, no matter how difficult it may be, the family must also be forgiving toward the one who tries to tear it apart. When someone causes us pain, we must try to apply the principle of Christ. Perhaps, as God's forgiveness has made a difference in our lives, it will make a difference in the troublemaker's life. As we are reminded by the scriptures, "Forgive each other, just as the Lord has forgiven you" (Col 3:13).

Compassion — Day 34

All of you, have unity of spirit, sympathy, love for one another, a tender heart, and a humble mind. (1 Pet 3:8)

I wish compassion could be scientifically measured, put into capsules, and prescribed for everyone to swallow at least four times a day. Or at least we could all have a vial of them to distribute whenever necessary.

I longed for such a miracle drug several years ago when I became involved with a group of women who met once a week for spiritual growth and development. The group spent several months searching for appropriate topics to discuss and finally settled into a kind of gossip circle that badmouthed poor, unsuspecting husbands.

Two women in particular relished the opportunity of discussing their mates in a negative light. They convinced themselves that their husbands had to undergo total transformations or face drastic consequences.

I knew the husbands. Maybe they were in a rut and a bit too complacent about their ways of life. But they were basically good, gentle men who did not deserve the fierce condemnation heaped upon them by their wives in our weekly meetings.

The wives made no attempt to understand their husbands' feelings. They merely fed each other's anger and bitterness, and fulfilled the psalmist's question, "Has he/she in anger shut up his/her compassion?" (Ps 77:9).

Take another example. In one of the churches my husband served as a minister, there was a thrift shop filled with used clothing and household articles donated for needy people. At a meeting in which the thrift shop was discussed, a woman asked why the prices were so high. She feared that a lot of "street-people" couldn't afford to pay them. The manager of the thrift shop answered without hesitation: "Oh, we keep the prices high to keep out the riff-raff."

Where, O where, I wondered, was that compassion pill? I wanted to remind the manager of a verse in Colossians: "As God's chosen ones, holy and beloved, clothe yourselves with compassion, kindness, humility, meekness, and patience" (Col 4:12a).

On another occasion in that same church, a festive party was in progress following a Sunday service. Platters were laden with sandwiches and holiday sweets, and the air was filled with joy and excitement. A dirty, raggedly dressed man wandered in off the street and approached one of the food tables. Swooping upon the situation like a hawk, one of the church elders grabbed up the platter of food from the table and said, "This is not for you!" The elder had so much, but the other man had so little. What happened to the elder's sense of compassion and justice?

The Bible gives us example after example of God's compassion and mercy, from God sparing the nation Israel after it had been stubborn and rebellious to the way Christ forgave the men who put him on the cross. Why can't we, in turn, remember to be generous and forgiving? We may not have a compassion pill to swallow, but our faith does prescribe an open and loving spirit. What positive results we get from that prescription! It makes all the difference in the world.

Words — Day 35

By your words you will be justified, and by your words you will be condemned. (Matt 12:37)

In *My Fair Lady*, an exasperated Eliza Doolittle says, "Words, words, words. All I ever hear is words." It can be mind-boggling to consider all the words we hear and use in a single day. But words are essential at every stage of life.

Infants respond to gentle words with smiles and coos.

Toddlers experiment with sounds and learn to use the words they hear from their parents and siblings.

Elementary school children spend a lot of time memorizing new words to expand their mental and emotional horizons.

Teenagers often mint their own vocabularies and sometimes develop selective deafness toward the words of older persons.

Young adults respond enthusiastically to certain words that are filled with promise and hope for them.

Middle-aged persons continue to have adventures with words, discovering their romance, impact, and individuality.

Older persons reflect on the words they have known and their associations with them, often with smiles and wonderment.

Words form a complete circle from the gentle beginning of life to its gentle ending. From the beginning to the ending, we experience an incredible torrent of words. Eliza was right. "Words, words, words"—countless numbers of words. What do we do with so many words?

Hopefully, we select them wisely, use them carefully, respect their value, profit from their repetition, give thanks for their beauty, and ponder their meaning. Prayerfully we repeat, "Let the words of my mouth and the meditation of my heart be acceptable to you, O Lord" (Ps 19:14).

Time   Day 36

> [They] would spend their time in nothing. (Acts 17:21)

Someone wrote, "Time misspent is not lived but lost." That is a frightening thought. How much of my life have I really lost, as surely as if I had not had it at all or as if it had been sucked down a dark hole somewhere?

I have wasted so much precious time on trivial matters—shopping for something I didn't need, reading a newspaper that didn't have anything of importance in it, or watching a T.V. show that was inane or pointless.

I have spent so many hours whimpering to myself over bad experiences, especially the rudeness or unkindness of others that made me feel unworthy or rejected. I have heard that people can't do anything to you that you don't allow them to do. At times, though, when my energy is low, my defenses are weak, and my self-esteem seems to have taken a vacation, I can't help feeling hurt. But what a waste of time it really is.

And all those hours worrying that I have misspent other hours! That's ironic, isn't it, spending time worrying about other time not well spent. I worry that I didn't fulfill my promise as a student. I worry that I wasn't as good a mother as I should have been. I worry that I didn't become the pianist I might have become. I worry that I haven't served God as I ought to have served.

My father used to talk about throwing good money after bad. Well, this is throwing good time after bad. I just can't seem to stop doing it. I want to live my time and not lose it. When am I really living time and not wasting it? When I am doing something for another. When I am learning and growing as a person. When I am consciously in the presence of God, feeding on divine love and grace.

I suppose it all comes down to being a good manager and not spending my time in the wrong ways. The Bible calls it "redeeming the time." I hope I can do it. I do so want to feel at peace before time runs out.

Justice — Day 37

O God, judge the earth. (Ps 82:8a)

According to Webster's New World Dictionary, justice means "fairness, reward or penalty, rightfulness, power to uphold what is right, to be tried in court and duly punished." But how justice is meted out depends on who is in charge of it. Justice can be good or bad, fair or unfair, soft or harsh, merited or unmerited. If it were left in the hands of God, there would be no cause for alarm, because God is always righteous. But justice can be problematic when human beings become the prosecutor, judge, and jury.

I don't have the compassion God has. I seldom see the whole picture—only the little part that affects me or people close to me. I tend to react with passion and prejudice when I think my space has been invaded or my rights violated.

Not too long ago, I received a letter from one of my aunts. She enclosed a card written by another aunt. The card contained some malicious gossip about a member of our family. It was not only malicious gossip, it was secondhand malicious gossip.

I confess I don't know how to handle things like that. I get all stirred up. The gossip was terribly unjust. How am I supposed to feel about it? What does my faith say that is relevant to such a situation? Did Jesus give a parable that would deal with it? Oh, I know we're not supposed to be anxious and we're supposed to forgive "seventy times seven" and all that. But, in the meantime, what happens to justice?

I began burning with indignation over injustice when I was only a child. A girl named Gwen and I exchanged pencil boxes in first grade. When I came home with a different box, my mother accused me of stealing it. I protested, but she didn't believe me. I was humiliated and filled with rage. I didn't steal the pencil box, and it was wrong to treat me as if I had.

My mother and father were always making me feel as if I had done something wrong. Sometimes I want to hold and rock that little girl who so often crouched by the bureau, afraid that the world would find out she was such a bad child. She lived with the words ringing in her ears, "You are guilty, you are guilty, you are guilty."

Now I still feel guilty, but I also feel outraged by injustice wherever it occurs. Having been made to feel guilty when I wasn't only increases my sense of rage. It is awful to live with a sentence of guilt when I am not actually guilty. I often think I've done something wrong when I have not. I wonder how others could love me. I even wonder how God could love me. I don't feel worthy of love.

The whole thing is complicated by this terrible sense of anger about injustice. I feel as if I am beating on an unscalable wall with clenched fists, crying out for justice in a world where there is none. I know what my problem is. I am still trying to be prosecutor, judge, and jury. I am trying to take God's place. God is the real prosecutor, judge, and jury—not I.

I keep praying for the day when I can turn all of these feelings over to God and hear God say, "Not guilty." Then, I suppose, I will feel that there is real fairness in the world and that I am fully and unconditionally accepted. When that time comes I will stop feeling rage about other injustice in the world. I will truly be at peace in myself, and I can become an agent of peace to others.

Independence   Day 38

> For freedom Christ has set us free. (Gal 5:1)

When one of our sons was beginning to talk in sentences, the words I seemed to hear most often were, "I do myself." If I started to hold a door for him, he said, "I do myself." If I offered to tie his shoelaces, he said, "I do myself." If I tried to comb his hair, he said, "I do myself." He was such a little man! That son grew up into a fine, competent adult, who still says in many ways, "I do myself." "You know me, Mom," he will say when I have offered to help him with something, "I have to do it myself." I still admire him for his independent spirit.

I wonder if we are sometimes too independent for our own good. I wish young people today could listen to their parents about things like sex and drugs. Many of them don't seem to realize that the parents aren't trying to manage their lives; they only want to impart some wisdom to the children that will save the children from grief and trouble. I wish older folks could accept help from their children without feeling that it is demeaning or that they will lose their independence. I wish we could all learn to rely on one another more than we do and feel a sense of joy in the good will of others when it is extended to us.

Accepting help when we need it is not a sign of weakness. In fact, it can often be a sign of intelligence. I have friends who complain that their husbands are too stubborn to stop and ask directions at a service station when they become lost while traveling. That seems silly to me. Why should people go in circles to prove their independence when a question or two could put them on the right track and save precious time for other things?

My husband was the pastor of a church where some people demonstrated their independence by never letting anyone else know when they were ill in the hospital. What wonderful opportunities for interaction and fellowship they missed! Some people didn't want news of deaths in the family announced so that others could call or visit, send flowers, and join them in the grieving process. They will never know what their sense of independence cost them!

I appreciate my independence as much as anyone; I hope I will never lose it. But I am also grateful for my interrelatedness to my family and friends and to the greater society beyond them. Life is too big for me to live it by myself. It was meant for sharing and caring.

Our son understands this now. He says he still likes to do things for himself, but that it is awfully comforting to know that Mom and Dad are there if he needs us. He tries not to call on us unless he has to, but he knows we are there. I feel the same way about God. I don't ask God for everything I need, a lot of things I can take care of myself. But it is reassuring to know I can call on my heavenly Father when I need to.

Faith — Day 39

Faith is the assurance of things hoped for, the conviction of things not seen. (Heb 11:1)

How frequently in my prayers these days I cry out for help, acknowledging the fact that I am lost and confused. For ten years, I was a minister's wife. Now my husband has returned to the classroom to teach, and my minister's-wife career has ended or been put on hold. I find myself floundering from a lack of identity, feelings of worthlessness, a sense of loneliness, and a shortage of faith. I feel abandoned, like a fish that has been washed up on the shore and can't get back to the sea. I'm impatient for answers. When will my life settle into normal routines again? When will I be happy again just being who I am?

When I was a child, I depended on my parents to care and provide for me. Then I grew up, married, and shifted my dependence to my husband. One day I realized that I was responsible for me. I began blossoming into a person on my own, capable of handling all kinds of situations. Faith in my parents, faith in my husband, faith in myself—but where did God fit into all of this? What about faith in God?

For years, I boasted that I relied on God for everything. But did I? If I did, why was I so afraid when I boarded an airplane? Why did I sit there with a list of scriptural texts in my hand:

- I am with you always. (Matt 28:20b.)
- The Lord is my light and my salvation, whom shall I fear? (Ps 27:1)
- Why are you afraid, you of little faith? (Matt 8:26)
- The Lord is my rock, my fortress, and my deliverer, my God, my rock in whom I take refuge. (Ps 18:2)

If I really relied on God, why was my faith so weak? Why is it so weak now? Why do I feel lost and confused?

Maybe that's the nature of faith. It isn't about getting over fear and confusion, only about coping with them. It's about having a name to call on when we're in despair. It's about calling out in the dark and knowing someone is there. Maybe that's the answer. I am floundering now, but I know there is a hand reaching out to me in the dark. One of these days, I will find it, and I won't be lost any more—not for a while. Then I will be lost again, and I will cry out again. Again the hand will be there. I can accept life like that. It gives me something to go on. I know I am never alone.

Beginning

Day 40

In the beginning . . . God created. (Gen 1:1)

When I was growing up, Easter was my favorite time of year. It always came when the earth was being reborn. Shoots were sprouting up all over my father's newly planted garden. Once-bare, winter tree limbs were adorned with brightly colored blossoms and waxy baby leaves. Birds were singing so cheerfully that all of their songs seemed new. The very air was fresh with the promise of good things ahead.

Although our family was relatively poor, my mother always saw that I had a new outfit to wear on Easter Day. She usually made my clothes and purchased small accessories from the department store. We would lay the pieces of the outfit on the bed and lovingly admire them. I was always so excited that I thought my skin wouldn't hold me!

At those times, the whole world seemed to be full of anticipation. Everything was aimed at that special day of celebration, when it would be trumpeted abroad that Christ was raised, and, because he lived, we too would live. I have never forgotten the sense of new beginning I always felt. It was as if the old slate of my life had been scrubbed clean, and I could start all over again. I wanted to sing and dance and fly with the angels.

Beginnings are wonderful:

- the beginning of the school year, when routine and discipline and learning take over again; the fun of ballgames, dances, dating; discovering a subject that opens new doors to life; sharing the laughter and excitement that echo in the halls

- the beginning of marriage, with its high hopes and dreams about to be fulfilled

- the beginning of family life, when children come into the home and all of our understanding is transposed into a new key

- the beginning of a new job, with all the new relationships and experiences it will entail

- the beginning of a new phase of life when we move from one place to another

Isn't it remarkable how many beginnings God has created for us? And then, one day, a shadow falls across all beginnings, and death stops them all. At least, that's what I thought until one day when our ten-year-old son corrected me.

One of my husband's colleagues died very suddenly. He was seated at his desk at the university and simply slumped over. When I heard the news, I began to cry. How sad it was, I thought, for his wife and children—for all of us. Our son saw the tears on my face. "Why are you crying, Mommy?" he asked. I tried to explain to him about our friend and the fact that he had died. "Oh Mommy," he said, "don't cry. Death is only the spawning of a new life." I looked at his sweet, young face. What wisdom it was hiding!

My son was right. Death is only another beginning—the most important one, in fact. Death is life with the Creator of everything, the Master of all new beginnings. In the end —was the beginning.